Over New Orleans

Over New Orleans

Aerial Photographs by David King Gleason

Foreword by Samuel Wilson, Jr.

DAVID KING GLEASON, PUBLISHER
BATON ROUGE, LOUISIANA

To my best friend, my wife, Josie

Copyright © 1983 by David King Gleason
Designer: Joanna Hill
Editor: Martha L. Hall
Typeface: Palatino
Typesetter: Moran Colorgraphic Incorporated
Printer and Binder: Dai Nippon Printing Company, Tokyo, Japan

LIBRARY OF CONGRESS CATALOGING IN PUBLICATION DATA
Gleason, David K.
    Over New Orleans
1. Historic Buildings—New Orleans, Louisiana—Pictorial Works
2. New Orleans—Louisiana—Pictorial Works.
3. Louisiana—Description and travel—1983—Views. I. Title

ISBN 0-9612038-0-3

The author gratefully acknowledges the assistance of the staff of Gleason Photography: Gisela O'Brien, who made the color prints for this book; associates Herman Robert, Donna Hall, Madeline Berggreen, research assistant Craig Saucier; and Mary Ewing, who kept us all on course.
    Aircraft were from Tigerland Aviation, pilot Richard McCray; Metro Aviation, pilot Bill Meier; Peterson Maritime Services, pilot Michael Chapman; and Louisiana Helicopter, pilot Jeff Ward.
    The bucket truck was from First Impression, and operated by Dennis Meyer and Jack LaPlante.

For information contact:
David King Gleason
1766 Nicholson Drive
Baton Rouge, Louisiana 70802
(504) 383-8989

Contents

Along the Bayous and the River

1. Pontchartrain Causeway
2. New Orleans International Airport
3. Bonnet Carré Spillway
4. Manchac Swamp
5. San Francisco
6. Manresa Retreat House
7. L' Hermitage
8. Madewood
9. Laurel Valley
10. Golden Meadow
11. Fort Livingston
12. Mouth of the Mississippi
13. Fort Jackson
14. Bayou Barataria
15. English Turn
16. Fort Pike
17. Chalmette Battlefield

Within the City

1. French Quarter
2. Faubourg Marigny
3. Central Business District
4. Superdome
5. Algiers Point
6. Garden District
7. Tulane and Loyola Universities
8. Audubon Park and Zoo
9. Carrollton
10. Notre Dame Seminary
11. Metairie Cemetery and Longue Vue Gardens
12. Yacht Basin
13. University of New Orleans and Southern University
14. City Park
15. Fairgrounds Racetrack
16. Dillard University
17. Bayou Metairie
18. Ochsner Institutions
19. Pontchartrain Causeway

Foreword

by Samuel Wilson, Jr., F.A.I.A.

The site of New Orleans was first seen and the course of the Mississippi River to its mouth in the Gulf of Mexico was first explored by Robert Cavalier, Sieur de la La Salle, in 1682. Above the head of the passes of the river's delta, La Salle set up a wooden cross and a column to which was attached a lead plate engraved with the arms of France and the following inscription (in French): "Louis the Great, King of France and of Navarre, reigns, the 9th April 1682." La Salle then proclaimed that "in the name of His Majesty and of the successors of his crown, I have taken and do take possession of this country of Louisiana."

Thus the name *Louisiana* was given to the vast area drained by the Mississippi and its tributaries. No attempt was made, however, to settle the area until the French-Canadian, Pierre Lemoyne, Sieur d'Iberville, led a small expedition to the Gulf Coast and established Fort Maurepas on Biloxi Bay in 1699. He entered the mouth of the river on March 2, and the next day gave the name Bayou Mardi Gras to a small outlet a short distance above the head of the passes, the first and most appropriate place name given by the French in Louisiana. The same expedition also named Lakes Pontchartrain and Maurepas in honor of the French minister of Marine and his son and successor as minister. Bayou St. John, which empties into Lake Pontchartrain and was connected to the Mississippi River by an old Indian portage, was named for Iberville's younger brother, Jean Baptiste Lemoyne, Sieur de Bienville. In 1718 Bienville founded the city of New Orleans where this portage met the river, naming it in honor of Philippe, Duc d'Orléans, then regent of France, uncle of the young King Louis XV. Bayou St. John, the lakes, and Mississippi Sound provided a sheltered water route to the earlier French settlement at Mobile.

Serious questions were raised from the beginning concerning the location of New Orleans, for the land along the river is low and flat and subject to flooding as the level of the river rises annually in the spring. Some advocated placing the city below English Turn, a great S-shaped bend in the river, a difficult stretch in the river for the sailing ships of the day to maneuver. Others thought that the city should be placed on the higher ground above Bayou Manchac near the site where Baton Rouge was later established. Bienville, however, adhered to his first choice at the Bayou St. John portage on what he regarded as one of the most beautiful curves on the lower river, a curve that gave the appellation *Crescent City* to New Orleans.

The plan of the city was designed by the engineer-in-chief of Louisiana, Pierre Leblond de la Tour, and laid out by his assistant, Adrien de Pauger, who began his work at the site on March 29, 1721. The town that he then laid out is now the Vieux Carré, or the French Quarter, of New Orleans, and most of its streets retain the names given to them at that time, names of saints interspersed with names of Bourbon princes. At the center of the plan at the top of the river bend was placed the public square or Place d'Armes (now Jackson Square) from which views up and down the river were possible, a baroque concept comparable to the plan of Versailles, where vistas from the palace forecourt extend along the great diagonal avenues of the town. Leblond de la Tour and Pauger were trained military engineers, and the New Orleans plan followed the gridiron pattern for a French fortified town.

No fortifications were actually built until 1760 when news reached New Orleans of the fall of Quebec to the English in the French and Indian War. As a result of France's defeat, all of Louisiana east of the Mississippi above Bayou Manchac was surrendered to England. Then Louis XV gave the rest of his Louisiana province, including New Orleans, to Spain. New fortifications, roughly following the line of the French palisade of the 1760, were erected by the Spanish governor, Louis Hector, Baron de Carondelet, in 1791. Napoleon retrieved Louisiana from Spain and sold it to the United States in 1803. The fortifications were soon demolished and replaced by the broad avenues of Canal Street, Rampart, and Esplanade that now bound the Vieux Carré on three sides.

The protection of New Orleans from foreign invasion caused the construction of a fort at the Balize near the mouth of the Mississippi in 1723. Later the French constructed Forts Bourbon and St. Philip at Plaquemines Bend on the lower river, forts later rebuilt under the American regime in the nineteenth century, Fort Bourbon renamed Fort Jackson. Farther upriver at English Turn, Forts St. Leon and St. Mary were constructed by the French in 1746, but little or no trace of them remains today. A small fort on Bayou St. John at the lake defended that approach to New Orleans, a fort rebuilt by Spain and later by the United States and still, as a ruin, known as Spanish Fort. After the thwarted British invasion of 1814–1815, the United States in 1818 built Forts Pike and Macomb on the Rigolets and the Chef Menteur passes between Lake Pontchartrain and Lake Borgne, as well as other forts in the area, all of which are now in ruins.

When news of the cession of Louisiana to Spain reached New Orleans, the first Spanish governor, Don Antonio de Ulloa, was driven from the colony in the first revolt against a European power in America. Carlos III of Spain sent a new governor, Don Alexander O'Reilly, with a contingent of troops, who suppressed the rebellion, tried and executed the leaders of the revolt, and sent others to prison. Thus Spanish rule was firmly established in Louisiana. A Cabildo was established as the city government in a small building next to the parish church facing the Plaza de Armas, on the site of the present imposing Cabildo building. Spain governed the colony well, but only the governor and a few officials represented the Spanish crown in New Orleans. The culture and language, except for official legal documents, remained French, as did the architecture.

The city prospered and grew under Spanish rule, but a large part of it was destroyed by two fires—one on March 21, 1788, which burned the Cabildo, the parish church and Presbytère, and a great number of buildings in the lower part of the city.

After the fire of 1788 the area above what is now Canal Street, then the plantation of Don Beltran Gravier, was laid out by Don Carlos Trudeau as the first suburb of the city. Named the Faubourg (suburb) Ste. Marie in honor of Gravier's wife, it extended upriver to about where Howard Avenue is today. Spain had supported the American Revolution, the Louisianians under Spanish Governor Don Bernardo de Gálvez driving the British from Baton Rouge, Natchez, Mobile, and Pensacola, and encouraged many Americans to come to Louisiana. After the Louisiana Purchase in 1803 many more Americans came to New Orleans, most of them settling in the Faubourg Ste. Marie, or St. Mary, which became known as the American Sector, separated from the French Quarter by Canal Street. This first suburb has become the Central Business District of modern New Orleans.

Napoleon Bonaparte took back Louisiana from Spain in 1801 and had ideas of re-creating a French empire in America. He appointed Pierre-Clément de Laussat as governor, but before Laussat reached Louisiana, Napoleon had sold the entire colony to the United States. On November 30, 1803, Laussat took formal possession from Spain, and on December 20, 1803, he transferred the vast Louisiana colony to the United States, which was represented by General James Wilkinson and its first American governor, William C. C. Claiborne. These formal ceremonies took place in the Sala Capitular on the upper floor of the Cabildo and in the public square (now Jackson Square) in front of it, where the tricolor of France was replaced by the stars and stripes of the United States.

Although many Americans moved into the new territory of Louisiana after the transfer, New Orleans remained essentially French for many years. Most of its people spoke French, and its newspapers were published in both French and English. A strong rivalry existed between the two segments of the population, but they were drawn together when the city was threatened by the invasion of the British troops in the War of 1812. The decisive defeat of the British under General Edward Pakenham by the Americans under General Andrew Jackson on the fields of the Chalmette plantation below New Orleans on January 8, 1815, brought a feeling of unity to the diverse elements of the population—Creoles, Americans, Free Negros, and black slaves.

The city grew rapidly in population and in wealth. After the successful granulation of sugar on a commercial basis by Etienne Boré in 1796, sugarcane became the principal crop in lower Louisiana. Indigo plantations soon became sugarcane plantations, and this, with the cotton crops farther up the river and the bountiful supply of timber, soon enabled New Orleans to become one of the busiest ports and one of the largest cities of the nation.

In 1805 the plantation of Bernard de Marigny below the city was subdivided as the Faubourg Marigny and was soon followed by other suburbs down and upriver. In 1806 the architect-surveyor Barthelemy Lafon laid out the Faubourg Annunciation, including such landmarks as Tivoli Circle (now Lee Circle), Annunciation Square, and Coliseum Place. Originally part of the plantation of the city's founder, Bienville, and from 1726 to 1763 part of the Jesuits' plantation, this area has in recent years become known as the Lower Garden District, extending as far up as Jackson Avenue.

The city of Lafayette was incorporated in 1833, and in 1852 this town became what is now known as the Garden District and the Irish Channel, settled by Americans but with large segments of German and Irish immigrants.

In the early 1830s the Macarty plantation was subdivided as the town of Carrollton, and in 1834 the New Orleans and Carrollton Railroad was built along what is now St. Charles Avenue to connect the new town of Carrollton to New Orleans. This provided access to lands away from the river and resulted in the development of the Garden District in the 1850s and early 1860s.

The Civil War temporarily halted the city's growth and prosperity, and the unhappy period of Reconstruction followed the war. Then came a new surge of building activity that saw the development of St. Charles Avenue as the city's principal residential street, where mansions were erected in the 1880s and 1890s and on into the twentieth century. St. Charles was and is still included in the routes of most of the major Carnival parades. Tulane University moved from its downtown location to a St. Charles Avenue site, opposite Audubon Park, in 1894. The park, designed by the noted landscape architects Olmstead Brothers of Boston, had been the site of the World's Industrial and Cotton Centennial Exposition of 1884. Loyola University, a Jesuit institution, located adjacent to Tulane facing St. Charles Avenue, and St. Mary's Dominican College and the Academy of the Sacred Heart are three other large educational institutions that were established along the avenue in the nineteenth century.

Before the financial crash of 1929, taller buildings than had ever been thought possible to erect on the alluvial soil of New Orleans were constructed. The Hibernia Bank building with its circular templelike tower, built in 1926, was for many years the tallest building in the city. Now many structures far exceed its height. Poydras Street, widened in the 1940s, is now lined with new buildings, including the huge Louisiana Superdome. The first bridge across the Mississippi River to link the east bank and Algiers on the west bank was opened in April, 1958, and now a parallel bridge is being constructed on its downriver side. The city has expanded to the shores of Lake Pontchartrain and is spreading to the east in new residential, commercial and industrial development.

The architecture that its French founders introduced to New Orleans was derived from France but influenced by what the French had previously done in Canada and in their West Indies possessions, principally St. Domingue (now Haiti). The French influence continued through Spanish rule and well into the nineteenth century.

The first buildings were simple frame structures built on wood sills placed on the ground, with walls of heavy timber studs called *colombage*, covered on the outside with wide horizontal boards. Their steeply pitched roofs were usually hipped and shingled. Soon galleries were added; brick foundations replaced the ground sills, and bricks or *bouzillage*, a mixture of mud and moss, was placed between the wall timbers for added stability and insulation; roof tiles replaced wood shingles on more important buildings. Houses were often built with a brick basement story and a second story of lighter weight colombage construction.

The only building that has survived almost intact from the period of French domination is the Ursuline Convent on Chartres Street, designed in 1745 by Ignace François Broutin. This is a fine example of the Louis XV style of the period, a two-story stuccoed brick building, the corners and frontispiece emphasized with rusticated quoins. The steep hipped roof, originally of flat tiles, is now of slate. The great cypress stairway with a wrought-iron railing in this old building was reused from the earlier convent of brick-between-posts that was build here in 1727–1734.

When Louisiana came under Spanish rule in the 1760s, no change was apparent in building design or construction, for the architects and builders, such as Guillemard, Lafon, Dujarreau, Boutee, and Trudeau, were all French. It was not until after the Corps de Garde, the Cabildo, parish church, and Presbytère facing the Plaza de Armas (now Jackson Square), and several hundred stores and houses were destroyed in the conflagration of 1788 that changes began to be made in building style and technique, for the frame construction and wood shingles of many buildings contributed to the rapid spread of the fire. The wealthy Spaniard Don Andrés Almonester y Roxas agreed to rebuild the parish church and Presbytère, and these new buildings were designed by the architect Don Gilberto Guillemard, born in France but for many years in the service of Spain. These two buildings were designed to have nearly flat tiled terrace roofs, which became a favorite roof form in the late eighteenth and early nineteenth centuries. Because it was almost impossible to keep such roofs from leaking, they were, for the most part, later covered over with more steeply pitched slate roofs.

One of the first private residences to be rebuilt after the 1788 fire was the house now known as "Madame John's Legacy" on Dumaine Street. This house was built for Don Manuel Lanzos, a Spanish officer. The builder was an American, Robert Jones, but the style and details of the house were in the earlier French tradition. After a second fire in 1794, city laws were enacted to require that the walls of buildings be covered with at least one inch of plaster or stucco, and roofs tiled.

Few houses of the Spanish colonial period remain. Among several on Royal Street are the two built for Vincent Rillieux, great-grandfather of the noted French artist Edgar Degas. One of these Rillieux houses is now Waldhorn's at 343 Royal Street, and the other is Brennan's restaurant at 417 Royal. They were probably designed by the architect Barthelemy Lafon. The Merieult House, built in 1792 and altered in the 1830s, now houses the Historic New Orleans Collection. The fine wrought-iron balcony railings executed by Marcelino Hernandez, who came from the Canary Islands, are perhaps the most important Spanish contribution to the architecture of New Orleans. Examples of Hernandez' craftsmanship are to be found on the Cabildo and on the Little Theatre building across St. Peter Street from the Cabildo.

Following the Louisiana Purchase in 1803, Americans moved into the former Spanish colony in great numbers, but the culture of the city and its architecture remained essentially French. In this postcolonial period, however, new American ideas were introduced. In 1807 the noted English-born American architect Benjamin Henry Latrobe designed a United States Custom House in the American federal style—red brick with white columns and trim and green blinds. When he came to New Orleans for the first time in 1819 to complete his waterworks project, left unfinished by the death of his son Henry in 1817, he admired the French buildings of the city and deplored the increasing use of red brick, saying "the French stucco the fronts of their buildings and often color them; the Americans exhibit their red staring brickwork, imbibing heat thro' the whole unshaded substance of the wall." Latrobe, like his son, died in New Orleans of yellow fever; his death on September 3, 1820, occurred only a week or two after the plans for his last design, the Louisiana State Bank, (now Manheim's at Royal and Conti) had been accepted.

Perhaps the best example of the continuance of the French style during this transitional period is the Girod House at St. Louis and Chartres streets, built in 1814 and attributed to the French architect Jean Hyacinthe Laclotte. This period also witnessed an increasing use of classical forms in columns and pilaster and of geometrical forms in buildings and ornament, notably in the simplified designs of wrought-iron balcony railings with diamonds, rectangles, and circles replacing the baroque scrolls and curves of the earlier Spanish ironwork.

By the 1830s, even such French Creole builders as Claude Gurlies and Joseph Guillot had begun to use red brick on the façades of their buildings, although retaining the French plan with a carriageway leading to a courtyard, and rooms opening into each other without a center hall. When Joseph LeCarpentier first planned his house on

Chartres Street opposite the old Ursuline Convent in 1826, there was to be no center hall, but later a new plan by the architect François Correjolles, whose parents were refugees from St. Domingue, provided for a center hall and pedimented portico. This fine house is now known as Beauregard House.

William Brand was outstanding among the American architect-builders who came to New Orleans after 1803. His most notable work, the house he built for Samuel Herman in 1831 (now the Christian Woman's Exchange), is typically American with a center hall and a symmetrical façade of brick, painted red and penciled. Two handsomely carved doorways open, one from the street and the other onto the wrought-iron balcony. Row houses such as the thirteen buildings of Julia Row of 1831 added to the Americanization of New Orleans architecture.

By 1835 the Greek Revival and other romantic revival styles—Gothic, Egyptian, Moorish, and Oriental—became popular in New Orleans as in other parts of the country. In that year William Strickland, pupil of Latrobe, designed the great Greek Revival style United States Mint, and in 1848 work was begun on the Egyptianesque United States Custom House on Canal Street, designed by Alexander Thompson Wood, who had come from New York about 1831 to build row houses. These two monumental federal buildings anchor the two river corners of the Vieux Carré.

The years between 1835 and the Civil War produced many of the city's most notable buildings. In the Vieux Carré, the French architect J. N. B. Depouilly in 1835 designed the St. Louis Hotel, inspired by the arcaded buildings along the Rue de Rivoli in Paris. The St. Louis was demolished in 1916, and its site is now occupied by the Royal Orleans Hotel. In the American Sector, above Canal Street, the Irish architect James Gallier and his New York partner Charles B. Dakin designed the magnificient St. Charles Hotel in the Greek Revival style, the dome of which dominated the city's skyline until it burned in 1851. It was rebuilt without the dome, burned again in 1896, and was replaced by a third hotel designed by the local architect Thomas Sully. It was demolished several years ago, and new buildings are now being erected on its site.

Rivalry continued to exist between the French and Anglo-American segments of the population. In the French Quarter, the Vieux Carré, the old Spanish cathedral, except for parts of its front wall, was demolished and a new and larger church, the present St. Louis Cathedral, was designed by Depouilly in 1850. French mansard roofs were added to the Cabildo and Presbytère in 1847, and in 1850 the Baroness Pontalba, Almonester's daughter, erected the rows of red brick buildings that bear her name, flanking the square now named Jackson Square. Plans for these buildings were first drawn by James Gallier and later revised by Henry Howard. It was on the Pontalba buildings that cast-iron galleries were first used in New Orleans.

Such ornate galleries were soon seen all over the city and have become almost symbolic of New Orleans.

In the American sector, St. Patrick's Church was built in 1839 in the Gothic Revival style by Charles Dakin and his brother, James, who had come down from New York. The interior of the church was completed by James Gallier after the Dakins were dismissed by the trustees. For many years its 185-foot tower was the tallest structure in New Orleans. In 1852 the Jesuit church on Baronne Street was built in a Moorish style with elaborate cast-iron interior columns and arches and even cast-iron pews. In 1850 Gallier completed the splendid Greek Revival city hall on Lafayette Square, a building that now bears his name.

The commercial center of the city gradually moved above Canal Street with numerous stores, offices, banks, and warehouses being erected in a variety of styles, many like the Custom House and the Canal Bank by Dakin having façades of Massachusetts granite. Others used cast iron in highly decorated façades and for ornamental window heads, columns, and other decorative elements. Large mansions were built in the Garden District in the 1850s and in the years following the Civil War, many of them making lavish use of cast iron in galleries, columns, and fences.

The 1880s and 1890s saw an increasing use of wood, turned and scrollwork decorative elements; doors, windows, brackets, and even entire façades could be ordered from catalogs. Low-cost "shotgun" and "camelback" houses were built in great numbers and embellished with these wood decorations. The shotgun is a long, narrow one-story house, often doubled, one room behind another, sometimes with additional rooms above in the rear to make it a camelback. In the late nineteenth and early twentieth centuries the Romanesque Revival, popularized by the Boston (Louisiana-born) architect Henry Hobson Richardson, became popular in New Orleans. St. Charles Avenue mansions, the first buildings of Tulane University, and the Howard Memorial Library and adjacent Confederate Memorial Hall were designed in this round-arch masonry style.

As elsewhere, the colonial revival style was the popular idiom in the years before World War I, and in the years following it, skyscrapers rose in the Central Business District in the eclectic styles of the period. After World War II another building boom took place and continues until now with a proliferation of hotels and office buildings, the Superdome, and the Rivergate and Exposition Building. Prosperity comes from the city's port, the petrochemical industries, and from the evergrowing tourist influx, which is expected to grow to unprecedented size in 1984 during the Louisiana World Exposition, now under construction along the warehouse district riverfront.

New Orleans has indeed changed through the years, changes dramatically apparent when the city and its environs are viewed from the air.

PART ONE

The Vieux Carré

Mississippi River at New Orleans, Circa 1851

The great crescent of the Mississippi River was a bustling port in the 1850s. It was in New Orleans that the steamboat met the sailing ship, making the Crescent City the port that served half the country.

In this 1850s view looking north toward Lake Pontchartrain in the background, the St. Louis Cathedral is across the river, at center right. From the cathedral and Jackson Square, proceeding upriver toward the left, is the United States Custom House, on the city's widest street, Canal. Note that the river is much closer to the Custom House than it is today. The American Sector, the Central Business District, is in the center of the picture, with Lafayette Square and the city hall and St. Patrick's Church at the upriver side of the Central Business District. The open space at center left is Coliseum Square, heart of what is now called the Lower Garden District.

In the foreground, at extreme right, is Harvey Castle, a Gothic plantation home, located on the site of the future Harvey Canal.

This hand-colored lithographic view of New Orleans, circa 1851, is by Asselineau after Bachmann.

Courtesy the Historic New Orleans Collection

New Orleans and the Mississippi River

Apparently the 1850 artist who drew the illustration on the opposite page took a few liberties with per-spective, but the great crescent of the Mississippi re-mains essentially the same. The Harvey Canal is at the bottom of the picture, in the center, and the Cen-tral Business District at center right. St. Charles Ave-nue parallels the river connecting the Central Business District, at right, with Carrollton at extreme right. The three large tree-covered boulevards that appear to intersect in the background are, left to right, Napoleon, Louisiana, and Washington ave-nues.

VIEW OF JACKSON SQUARE. NEW ORLEANS.

Drawn by J. Dürler

Published & Lith. by Pessou & Simon. 161 Chartres St. N.O.

Jackson Square in the 1850s in a hand-colored litho-
graph by Pessou and Simon after Durier

Courtesy the Historic New Orleans Collection

Jackson Square, 1983 (right)

4

Cabildo, St. Louis Cathedral, Presbytère

Dominating Jackson Square, the focal point of the Vieux Carré, is St. Louis Cathedral. St. Louis is one of the oldest cathedrals in the United States and the third building to be erected on this site. The earliest, a temporary structure, just around the corner, was leveled by a hurricane in 1722, only four years after the colony was founded. The first church on this site burned about seventy-five years later and was rebuilt as a cathedral, along with the Cabildo, left, and the Presbytère, right, with funds provided by Don Andrés Almonester y Rojas.

Pirate's Alley separates the cathedral from the Cabildo, which housed the governing body for the city, and where, in a second-floor room the United States was ceded possession of the Louisiana Territory in 1803. To the left of the Cabildo is St. Peter Street, which intersects Chartres in the foreground.

The Presbytère, originally intended to be a residence for the clergy serving the parish church, was not completed until 1813. It was eventually used by the state courts.

Behind the cathedral is the Cathedral Garden, also called St. Anthony's Square in memory of·a rector of the cathedral, Antonio de Sedella, who came to Louisiana from Spain in 1779 and served until his death in 1829. Père Antoine's Alley, also named for the priest, separates the church from the Presbytère, which along with the Cabildo and the Louisiana State Arsenal immediately behind it, is part of the Louisiana State Museum complex.

Jackson Square and Pontalba Buildings (right)

On either side of Jackson Square, known as the Plaza d'Armas when the colony was a Spanish possession, are the Pontalba buildings, erected in 1850 by the Baroness Micaela de Pontalba, daughter of Don Almonester. Although called apartments, they are actually townhouses, each with its own courtyard and service wing. The downriver structure, in the foreground, is a Louisiana State Museum property; the one across the square is owned by the city of New Orleans.

Jackson Square, Toward River

Between Jackson Square and the Mississippi River (at top) is Washington Artillery Park, with its fountains and an elevated walkway across the levee to the riverbank. The brewhouse of the former Jackson Brewing Company (Jax Beer) and the paddlewheel tour boat, the *Natchez,* are in the background. The river, particularly in the spring, is higher than the surrounding land, and is held in check only by the levee.

French Market (right)

On Decatur Street the old French Market extends for six blocks downriver from Jackson Square and still offers a colorful mixture of fish, meat, and vegetables. The meat market, the "Halle des Bouchèries," whose terra-cotta roof dominates the foreground, is now a complex of tourist-oriented shops and coffeehouses.

Quarter, Downriver

In the foreground, occupying a city block between Royal and Chartres streets, is the former New Orleans Civil Courts Building, completed in 1909. Facing the court building, which later housed the Louisiana Department of Wildlife and Fisheries, the Royal Orleans Hotel, built on the site of the old St. Louis Hotel in 1963, incorporates a granite arcade from the original building.

New construction is permissible in the Vieux Carré only where there is a vacant lot, or where a business has been discontinued. In the Quarter, there is a height limitation of fifty feet on alterations and new construction, regulated by the Vieux Carré Commission.

Cathedral Garden and Royal Street, Upriver
(right)

Hidden by the trees in the Cathedral Garden, just behind St. Louis Cathedral, the rear of which is at left, is a statue erected by Napoleon III's minister of the navy honoring the memory of thirty French sailors from the steam corvette *Tonnerre,* who died of yellow fever during one of the many epidemics that plagued New Orleans until the advent of the twentieth century.

On the weekends, Royal Street, which the garden faces, is now a pedestrian mall.

Royal Street, Toward Central Business District

Not from a helicopter, but from the boom of a truck crane, the camera captures a more intimate view of Royal Street. Looking upriver toward the Central Business District is the American Sector.

Although Royal is one of the busiest streets in the Quarter, it has not a single traffic light. In fact, there are no traffic lights in the Vieux Carré.

In the city's earliest days, its streets were quagmires after the rains, which come almost daily during the summer. The sidewalks were elevated, as on the banks of a stream, hence the term *banquette*, which is still used.

Lafitte's Blacksmith Shop (right)

Lafitte's Blacksmith Shop, on the corner of Bourbon and St. Philip, is said to be one of the oldest buildings in the French Quarter, but the exact date of construction is unknown.

According to legend, the Lafitte brothers, pirates by profession, operated this smithy as a cover for their smuggling operations, although they were headquartered in the swamps south of the city along Bayou Barataria.

600 Block of Bourbon and Royal, Toward River

Within the block bordered by St. Peter Street at left, Bourbon in the foreground, Royal Street at the top, and Toulouse, right, is the Court of Two Sisters, a restaurant, which may be entered from either Royal or Bourbon and can be identified by the red and yellow umbrellas toward the lower right of the block. At its left is the courtyard of Pat O'Brien's Bar, entered from St. Peter Street.

Along Chartres Street (right)

Looking uptown toward St. Louis Cathedral from just below St. Philip Street along Chartres. The Central Business District is in the background.

Ursuline Convent and Beauregard House

Facing each other across Chartres Street are the Beauregard House and garden, at left, and the Ursuline Convent, the large structure in the center, which originally faced toward the river, several more blocks to the right.

Beauregard House Garden (right)

Across Chartres Street from the Ursuline Convent is the LeCarpentier House, better known as Beauregard House, and its garden. The house was built by Joseph LeCarpentier in 1827, on land bought from the Ursuline order, but acquired its present name when Confederate General P. G. T. Beauregard rented a room there following the Civil War. Others who enjoyed the garden were chess master Paul Morphy, born in 1837, whose grandfather was Joseph LeCarpentier, and Frances Parkinson Keyes. The novelist, who rebuilt the garden, restored the house, made it her winter residence, and established it as a museum.

Ursuline Convent and Beauregard House

Directly across Chartres from Beauregard House is Ursuline Convent, designed in 1745, completed in 1750, with a circular stair from an earlier 1734 convent, and said to be the oldest building in the Mississippi Valley. The great fire of 1788 destroyed most of the French colonial buildings of New Orleans except the convent, stopping at its walls.

Now known as the Archbishop Antoine Blanc Memorial, the six-building group houses the archives of the Catholic Archdiocese of New Orleans. Just beyond the garden in front of the main building is Our Lady of Victory Church, built in 1845, and formerly called St. Mary's Italian Church.

Flea Market and Old United States Mint (right)

At the downriver end of the French Market, along North Peters, the farmers' market, built by the WPA in the 1930s, offers a large variety of fresh fruits and vegetables from its rows of stalls beneath the long sheds extending from the market toward the United States Mint, in the background.

Now, on the weekends, the lower end of the farmers' market becomes a flea market, offering an even larger variety of things handmade, machine-made, inanimate and not.

Upriver Along Decatur (left) and Chartres

The Vieux Carré was originally bounded by the river and fortifications extending along Canal, Rampart, and Esplanade. Where Esplanade meets the river, stood Fort San Carlos in the 1700s, and in 1835 the United States Mint, lower left, was built facing Esplanade.

Now a part of the Louisiana State Museum, the mint produced $5 million in coin per month at its peak periods of operation, from 1838 to 1862, and from 1879 to 1910.

Esplanade and Elysian Fields Toward Lake Pontchartrain (right)

Just downriver from the Vieux Carré, is the city's second suburb, Faubourg (suburb) Marigny. Since the Mississippi makes a wide turn at this point, Marigny's streets, although paralleling and running perpendicular to the river, join those of the Quarter at an obtuse angle.

From above the warehouses at the water's edge looking toward Lake Pontchartrain, the United States Mint is in the lower left corner, fronting Esplanade, the long tree-shaded boulevard that runs from the river to City Park. The wide boulevard at the right, which intersects Esplanade at about 45 degrees, is Marigny's major street, Elysian Fields, which extends from the Mississippi to Lake Pontchartrain at the amusement park.

Washington Square in Faubourg Marigny

In 1800 Count Bernard de Marigny de Mandeville became probably the richest teen-ager in America when he inherited his father's vast plantation acreage. This centered on Marigny plantation, just downriver from the Vieux Carré. Subdivided in 1805 to form Faubourg Marigny, the new suburb focused on Washington Square, donated by Marigny. The square is the only one in New Orleans that has a double row of live oaks, and a wrought- and cast-iron fence on a granite base.

In the foreground is Elysian Fields Avenue, originally the Marigny Canal, which began at a sawmill at the edge of the river and continued toward Lake Pontchartrain.

In the background, the upper left corner, is Esplanade.

Gauche House Courtyard (right)

Facing Esplanade on Royal Street is one of the most impressive mansions in New Orleans, built by John Gauche in 1856. Gauche was a prosperous New Orleans merchant in the mid-nineteenth century, owning real estate, a warehouse, and the Gauche Crockery Company.

The house changed hands a number of times until it was purchased and restored in 1937 by Mrs. Matilda Geddings Gray, whose niece, Mrs. Harold Stream, undertook another restoration in 1967. The architectural firm of Koch and Wilson did both restorations.

The mansion itself is at the right, with the dependencies at left and center. The original kitchen was on the first floor behind the house, and has been replaced by a modern kitchen at the same location.

From St. Louis Cemetery No. 2 Toward Vieux Carré and River

In the foreground, paralleling Interstate-10, is the second oldest cemetery in New Orleans, St. Louis Cemetery Number 2, established in 1823.

Between St. Louis No. 2 and St. Louis No. 1, in about the center of the picture, is the Iberville Housing Project, which covers the approximate area of Storyville, New Orleans' famed redlight district of the turn of the century.

St. Louis Cemetery No. 1, Basin Street, and Our Lady of Guadeloupe Church (right)

Just across Basin Street (the green boulevard toward the French Quarter from St. Louis No. 1) is Our Lady of Guadeloupe church, built in about 1826 as a burial chapel for the two St. Louis cemeteries. Since the cause of the plagues was unknown at the time, funerals themselves were suspect as a source of contagion, and were forbidden by the city council to be held in the cathedral.

St. Louis Cemetery, established in 1788, was built well beyond the confines of the city. Since the water table in New Orleans is so close to ground level, graves dug in the traditional European manner quickly filled with water, making the burial of a coffin difficult. Before the development of the current practice of above-ground, plaster-covered brick tombs, holes were bored in the bottom of the coffin, and slaves stood on top, weighting the casket down with ballast stones until it sank beneath the water.

Canal Street

Flanking the Vieux Carré on the upriver side is Canal Street, which was never a canal but the proposed location of one that would have linked the turning basin on Basin Street with the Mississippi River.

Canal Street became the boundary separating the French Quarter from the American Sector (Faubourg Ste. Marie), established after the Louisiana Purchase. It literally was neutral territory between the two municipalities, and the middle ground in New Orleans boulevards is still called the "neutral ground."

The French Quarter is to the left in this view, and the Central Business District is at the right.

United States Custom House (right)

Now overshadowed by skyscrapers on either side, the United States Custom House, the third to be built on that site, was considered at the time of its construction the second largest public building in the country, surpassed only by the Capitol in Washington. Under construction between 1848 and 1881, its work was interrupted by the Civil War, and for some years thereafter.

Its Marble Hall is considered one of the finest Greek Revival interiors, measuring 95 by 125 feet, with a 54-foot ceiling.

When construction began, the river was much closer. In the colonial period, the levee was on the river side of North Peters, the street to the right of the Custom House in this photograph.

New Orleans Civil Courts Building, Royal Orleans Hotel, and Girod House

The New Orleans Civil Courts building is at left center, and Chartres Street separates it from the Royal Orleans Hotel at right.

Across Conti Street from the Royal Orleans is the Mayor Nicholas Girod house, with its octagonal cupola. Legend has it that the house was offered as a retreat for Napoleon, who was then in exile, but who died before the plan could be implemented.

The house is said to be similar to townhouses built in France at about that same time. The roof is one of the few in the Vieux Carré that still has its original tiles.

PART TWO

The Central Business District and Uptown

From Algiers Point Toward Central Business District

Algiers Point, in the foreground, was annexed by the city of New Orleans in 1870, but still has retained its nineteenth-century character. Now a Historic District bounded by the river on two sides, the town is highlighted by its turreted courthouse, which faces the parking lot of the Algiers–Canal Street ferry. A ferry has been in continuous operation here since 1827.

Foot of Canal Street (right)

At the foot of Canal Street, left, is the International Trade Mart, topped by a revolving cocktail lounge. Between the Trade Mart and the river is the Plaza de España. Behind the mart, which houses many offices of the city's maritime industry and the Louisiana Maritime Museum, is the Rivergate Exhibition Center, which has stimulated the construction of a number of nearby hotels. At right is the Algiers ferry and its landing. Beyond the ferry is the carrier *Lexington*.

Rivergate and Surrounding Hotels

In the center is the Rivergate Exhibition Center, the main hall of which provides 132,000 square feet of convention space, and which is operated by the Board of Commissioners of the Port of New Orleans.

Encircling the Rivergate are, clockwise from 12:00, the International Trade Mart; the Hilton, Sheraton, International and Marriott hotels; and One Canal Place, an office building.

Beyond the Hilton, looking upriver, are the site of the 1984 World's Fair and the Greater New Orleans Bridge, with its new parallel span, under construction.

From River Toward Central Business District
(right)

From just downriver from the Greater New Orleans Bridge, a freighter is steaming upriver past other ships at the docks near the Central Business District. Behind the docks is the site for the 1984 World's Fair, whose main exhibition hall is under construction at the left.

Rivergate and Surrounding Hotels

In the center is the Rivergate Exhibition Center, the main hall of which provides 132,000 square feet of convention space, and which is operated by the Board of Commissioners of the Port of New Orleans.

Encircling the Rivergate are, clockwise from 12:00, the International Trade Mart; the Hilton, Sheraton, International and Marriott hotels; and One Canal Place, an office building.

Beyond the Hilton, looking upriver, are the site of the 1984 World's Fair and the Greater New Orleans Bridge, with its new parallel span, under construction.

From River Toward Central Business District
(right)

From just downriver from the Greater New Orleans Bridge, a freighter is steaming upriver past other ships at the docks near the Central Business District. Behind the docks is the site for the 1984 World's Fair, whose main exhibition hall is under construction at the left.

From Central Business District to Superdome

In 1788, following the Good Friday fire, which destroyed a large part of the Vieux Carré, Madame Dona Maria Josefa Gravier and her husband Don Beltran Gravier retained the Spanish royal surveyor, Carlos Laveau Trudeau, to subdivide their plantation, which was located just upriver from the stricken city.

Development of the new Faubourg Ste. Marie did not proceed at a record pace for the first forty years, but by the 1830s, Canal Street (extending diagonally across the lower righthand corner) had become a stately thoroughfare, with Greek Revival "temples" on either side. But beyond Canal (looking toward the Superdome) it was little better than a marsh.

Within the next thirty years, from 1830 to 1860, New Orleans experienced its golden era, and the American Sector rapidly outstripped the French Quarter, becoming the vital, dynamic Central Business District.

Loyola Avenue and City Hall (right)

A continuation of Basin Street on the upper side of Canal, Loyola Avenue is on land that once was a part of a colonial plantation owned by the Jesuit order.

On the right side of the street is the Civic Center, with the City Hall facing Duncan Plaza. Behind the complex is a cluster of hotels that face the Superdome, which is just out of sight to the right.

From Superdome Toward Lake Pontchartrain

To the left of the Superdome was the turning basin for the New Basin Canal, which extended to Lake Pontchartrain, and whose right-of-way is now occupied by Pontchartrain Expressway, which enters this photograph from the left and continues toward the lake. Passing under the expressway just beyond the dome is Claiborne Avenue, and Interstate-10, curving in from the east, intersects a bit farther on.

The Superdome, 273 feet high, has a 680-foot diameter and is the world's largest room without posts. It seats about 76,000 for football games, and can handle over 100,000 in a festival configuration.

Dixie Brewery (right)

Toward Lake Pontchartrain from the Superdome, on Tulane Avenue, is the Dixie Brewery, the last survivor of thirteen locally owned breweries in New Orleans. The original building was constructed in 1907, when the brewery was founded.

In recognition of its efforts to compete with huge out-of-state brewers, the Louisiana legislature granted it a tax exemption to help Dixie continue its traditional brew.

From Superdome Toward River

The Superdome's grounds cover more than thirteen acres, which are now flanked by an expanding complex of office buildings and hotels. Directly behind the dome in this view is the Hyatt Regency, whose parent corporation also manages the Superdome.

The tallest building on the skyline is One Shell Square: fifty-one stories, 697 feet high, on Poydras Street, which runs toward the river from just left of the Superdome.

From River Side of Camp Street Toward Central Business District

The oldest church building in New Orleans, St. Patrick's Church, in the foreground facing Camp Street, was for many years the tallest building upriver from Canal Street. One block away from the church was the focal point of Faubourg Ste. Marie, Lafayette Square (the green area just beyond the church in this view).

St. Patrick's has now lost its original congregation, the Irish-Americans who came to town following the Louisiana Purchase, but it is maintained by visitors and members of other parishes who still hold strong bonds of affection for the old church, one of America's finest examples of the Gothic Revival style.

Lafayette Square and Federal Buildings

Lafayette Square was originally planned to be the centerpiece of Faubourg St. Mary. Facing this still-green area in the midst of the Central Business District are federal court buildings and the former city hall, now known as Gallier Hall, a Greek Revival structure in the lower left corner.

Facing Gallier Hall is a bronze statue of John Mc-Donogh, the benefactor of the New Orleans public school system. The center of the square is dominated by a bronze of Henry Clay, which was originally placed at the intersection of St. Charles and Canal in 1856, and moved to Lafayette Square in 1900.

Across the square from Gallier Hall is the Hale Boggs Federal Building and United States Court House, a contemporary structure; and to its right, the former United States Post Office, built in 1912, now housing the United States Court of Appeals, Fifth Circuit. At extreme right is St. Patrick's Church. On the right side of the square is the F. Edward Hebert Federal Building.

Thirteen Sisters of Julia Street (right)

In the 1830s and 1840s, Julia Street was one of the Crescent City's most exclusive areas, and it was near Camp Street, St. Patrick's Church, and the new city hall on Lafayette Square that architect Alexander Thompson Wood, designer of the Custom House a few years later, placed the Julia Row, or "Thirteen Sisters," in 1831, a delicately detailed group of thirteen red brick row houses, which predate the Pontalba buildings on Jackson Square by about twenty years.

At lower right is the former headquarters building for the Lighthouse for the Blind.

Lee Circle, Howard Avenue, and Confederate Museum

Called Tivoli Place before the erection of Robert E. Lee's monument in 1878, Lee Circle and its surroundings are surveyed by a statue of the beloved Confederate general, which stands atop a sixty-foot shaft of Tennessee marble.

Circling the statue in this view, which looks toward the river, is one of the St. Charles Avenue streetcars. The St. Charles Line, on the National Register of Historic Places, is the oldest continuously operated street railway line in the world.

Starting in 1835 as the Carrollton Line of the New Orleans and Carrollton Railroad, the line was powered by horse, mule, and steam before its electrification in 1893.

Facing Howard Avenue, directly above the streetcar, is an ivy-covered building that originally housed Howard Library, donated by Miss Annie T. Howard. The library has since moved to the Tulane University campus, and the building now houses law offices. Directly behind the Howard Library building, facing Camp Street, is the Confederate Museum housed in Confederate Memorial Hall, which was built and donated to the Louisiana Historical Association in 1893 by Frank T. Howard.

Coliseum Square and Lower Garden District (right)

Between the Garden District and the Central Business District is the Lower Garden District, an area distinguished by its collection of imposing Greek Revival and mid-Victorian houses of the 1850s and 1860s. Its focal point is Coliseum Square, which isn't square at all, and facing which was supposed to be a coliseum (more like the one in Paris of the 1770s, a dance hall for the middle classes), which was never built.

Garden District and Lafayette Cemetery

From high above New Orleans, Lafayette Cemetery, the white square in the center foreground, is a prominent landmark in the center of the Garden District, an area once known as the city of Lafayette, incorporated in 1833.

St. Charles Avenue, a wider, tree-shaded boulevard, runs diagonally across the lower lefthand corner toward the Central Business District. Paralleling St. Charles, but on the river side of the cemetery, is Coliseum Street, which extends upward in this picture toward Coliseum Square, directly below the Greater New Orleans Bridge.

Between the Garden District and the river is the area known as the Irish Channel, so named after its first inhabitants, Irish immigrants escaping the potato famines of the Emerald Isle in the first part of the nineteenth century.

The Channel had a considerable influence upon the development of Dixieland Jazz. The members of the Original Dixieland Jazz Band, first to make a recording, and the first to tour Europe, were born and reared in the Irish Channel.

Colonel Short's Villa in Garden District (right)

Completed just before the Civil War for a Kentucky colonel, Robert Henry Short, a wealthy commission merchant, this handsome Italian villa was designed by Henry Howard, the same architect who designed Belle Grove and Nottoway plantation homes, which vied for size and ornamentation with his villa.

Colonel Short enjoyed his house for only a brief time before it was seized by the Union commander who made it his headquarters after the fall of New Orleans in 1862.

Bordering the house and gardens is a cast-iron fence similar to that of the Cornstalk Hotel in the French Quarter.

Lafayette Cemetery

One of the oldest planned cemeteries in New Orleans, and one of the oldest above-ground cemeteries in the country, Lafayette Cemetery No. 1 was established in the city of Lafayette (annexed by New Orleans in 1852) in 1833.

The cemetery is the resting place for many German and Irish victims of yellow fever epidemics, and contains plots and vaults owned by some of the most prominent families in New Orleans.

In the distance, looking downriver, is the Central Business District, and at the right, across Washington Street from the cemetery, is the restaurant Commander's Palace.

Jackson Avenue in Garden District (right)

Facing Jackson Avenue in the Garden District is Trinity Episcopal Church, completed in 1853. In 1855 the first bishop of Louisiana, Leonidas Polk, a West Point graduate, became rector of the church, although he had been named bishop of the Episcopal diocese in 1841. At Jefferson Davis' request, Bishop Polk joined the Confederacy at the outset of the Civil War. General Polk was killed by a cannonball in 1864 at Pine Mountain, Georgia.

Across Jackson Avenue is one of the largest houses in the Garden District, the Buckner House, built in 1856, and now housing Soulé Business College. The house was designed by Lewis Reynolds, who was also the architect for Stanton Hall in Natchez.

Louise McGehee School

Distinguished by one of the most impressive spiral staircases in New Orleans, the mansion constructed for Bradish Johnson in 1872 is the main building for the Louise McGehee school, a girls' preparatory school, which acquired the property in 1929.

Sacred Heart Academy (right)

Located on St. Charles Avenue, farther uptown than the Garden District, is the Academy of the Sacred Heart. Opened in 1899, the school for girls is operated by members of the French religious order Madames of the Sacred Heart, who came to Louisiana in 1818 to open a convent and girls' school in the French Quarter. In 1887 the order purchased twenty-eight squares of land, an orange plantation, on St. Charles Avenue. The nuns opened the school in the existing plantation house and two years later began construction of the new school building.

Tulane and Loyola Universities and Audubon Park

In the cluster of buildings near the upper end of St. Charles Avenue are Loyola, right, the largest Catholic university in the South, and, left, Tulane University. In 1884 Paul Tulane contributed $1.1 million to the University of Louisiana, founded 1845, with the stipulation that it be restructured as Tulane University of Louisiana. In 1886 the first college for women within a university, the H. Sophie Newcomb Memorial College, was added to the Tulane complex.

Across St. Charles from Tulane and Loyola is Audubon Park, a 247-acre site that was purchased by the city in 1871. There New Orleans held the World's Industrial and Cotton Centennial Exposition in 1884–1885.

Audubon Place (right)

Adjacent to Tulane University on its upriver side is a prestigious New Orleans residential street, Audubon Place. The imposing Colonial Revival mansion on the left hand corner is the official residence of the president of Tulane.

Samuel Zemurray bought the house in 1917, about ten years after it was built by William T. Jay, whose English father had founded a Louisiana lumber empire. Zemurray, director of the United Fruit Company, made numerous bequests to Tulane, including the house, and established the Middle American Research Institute of Tulane University.

Audubon Park

On the grounds of what was to become Audubon Park, the World's Industrial and Cotton Centennial Exposition was opened on December 16, 1884. Although the city and the South still suffered from the effects of the Civil War and Reconstruction, the Exposition's promoters staged a world's fair that was said to have surpassed the efforts of far larger cities.

The lagoon in the foreground was created for the fair, which also featured Horticultural Hall, a 194-by-600-foot house of glass, the largest conservatory in the world at that time.

Audubon Park was designed in 1911 by Frederick Law Olmsted, who was the architect of Central Park in New York City.

Audubon Park Zoo (right)

River and Boat Landing at Audubon Park

Eastward from the boat landing and the river over-look on the banks of the Mississippi at Audubon Park is the Audubon Zoo, and in the distance, the Superdome and the Central Business District.

St. Mary's Dominican College (right)

St. John the Baptist School for Girls opened in New Orleans in 1860, and the following year was chartered under the name of New Orleans Female Dominican Academy. In 1865 the school purchased its present site.

The administration building, Greenville Hall, right center, was constructed in 1882 and is on the National Register of Historic Places.

Uptown Square

In contrast to the nearby Greenville Hall of Dominican College, Uptown Square is New Orleans' newest shopping center, completed in the fall of 1982.

The railroad tracks in the foreground, which parallel the levee, are part of the New Orleans Public Belt Railroad.

Carrollton Courthouse (right)

In 1835, Carrollton, at the uptown end of Nyades Street (now St. Charles Avenue) was a separate municipality, and at one point was the seat of Jefferson Parish after New Orleans had annexed Faubourg Lafayette.

Facing Carrollton Avenue, near its intersection with St. Charles, is the Greek Revival Carrollton Courthouse, designed by Henry Howard and built in 1854. Although it now serves as the Benjamin Franklin School, it still is a reminder of the days when the incorporated town four and a half miles upriver from New Orleans was the parish seat.

Notre Dame Seminary

Built in 1923, and designed by Colonel Allison Owen, Notre Dame Seminary is the first archdiocesan seminary to serve the New Orleans area, and offers a Master of Divinity degree. In the lower left corner is St. Joseph Hall, part of which is the seminary auditorium. Another section contains dormitories.

The smaller building to the right of the seminary is the residence for the archbishop, whose headquarters are in the white building at the rear, facing Walmsley Drive. Behind the headquarters building, in the upper left, is the Chateau de Notre Dame, a nursing home for the elderly.

Longue Vue House and Gardens (right)

Although a twentieth-century home, Longue Vue House was built in the classical tradition, recalling the great country houses of England.

Built by Edith and Edgar B. Stern, the house and gardens are now operated by the Longue Vue Foundation, which sponsors a series of horticultural workshops, lectures, and exhibitions on architecture, decorative arts, and landscape gardening throughout the year.

Metairie Cemetery

Near the intersection of Canal Boulevard and Metairie Road is a complex of cemeteries, one of which,

Metairie Cemetery, is laid out in an oval fashion. This is said to be the most elegant of the New Orleans burial grounds, chartered in 1872.

The site of the once famous Metairie Race Course, local legend has it that an American who was refused membership in the exclusive Louisiana Jockey

Club vowed to turn the track into a cemetery, hence the oval streets.

PART THREE

The Lakefront and Bayou St. John

New Basin Canal

By 1832 the Americans in Faubourg St. Mary, across Canal Street from the Creoles in the Vieux Carré, decided to build their own canal leading from Lake Pontchartrain into their own municipality.

The French establishment had enjoyed the commercial benefits of a canal from the lake to the Vieux Carré since 1796, when Baron de Carondelet ordered the construction of a canal from Bayou St. John to the rear of the city near Rampart Street.

The American project was to terminate in a turning basin near the Union Passenger Terminal, within a few blocks of the Superdome, and was promptly dubbed the New Basin Canal. It took six years, a million dollars, and the lives of eight thousand Irish laborers to finish the six-mile project. A popular resort and park developed in the 1880s at the lake end of the canal, now known as West End. In the 1940s the canal, except for a few hundred feet at the lake end, was filled in.

Lakefront (right)

Subdivisions along Lakeshore Drive are built on acreage reclaimed in the 1930s by the Orleans Levee Board. In the center is the Orleans Outfall Canal. At the rear, looking west toward Metairie, is the yacht basin, where the New Basin Canal joined the lake.

Yacht Basin and Orleans Marina

On the western side of the New Basin Canal at Lake Pontchartrain is the Yacht Basin of the Southern Yacht Club, organized in 1849, the second oldest in the United States. The white columns of the club building may be seen in the background.

Southern Yacht Club and Coast Guard Lighthouse (right)

The red roofed United States Coast Guard Lighthouse has overseen mariners on the New Basin Canal almost since its inception. Across the canal is the Southern Yacht Club.

Southern University in New Orleans

Beyond Wesley Barrow Baseball Stadium near the lakeshore is Southern University in New Orleans, founded in 1959. The 1983 enrollment was 2,800.

Pontchartrain Beach and University of New Orleans (right)

At the Lake Pontchartrain end of Elysian Fields Avenue, which leads on a straight line to Faubourg Marigny, immediately downriver from the Vieux Carré, is Pontchartrain Beach, an amusement park said to be one of the largest and best equipped in the United States.

Behind and to the right of Pontchartrain Beach is the campus of the University of New Orleans, founded as the New Orleans campus of Louisiana State University in 1956. The commuter college has a current enrollment of over 15,000.

Bayou St. John at Lake Pontchartrain

A few blocks west of Pontchartrain Beach is the entrance of a historic waterway to New Orleans, Bayou St. John.

The bayou allowed easy access to the great crescent on the Mississippi, which became the location for the Vieux Carré.

The earliest settlers in the New Orleans area built their homes along the bayou in 1708, ten years before the city was founded.

Golf Course, City Park (right)

Bayou St. John, which enters the picture at upper left, marked the eastern boundary of the Allard plantation, where, between 1891 and the 1930s, City Park was developed. The golf course is at right, and the Central Business District is in the background.

St. Louis Cemetery No. 3 and Fairgrounds Racetrack

Across Bayou St. John from City Park is St. Louis Cemetery No. 3, built on high ground along the bayou after the first two St. Louis cemeteries near the Vieux Carré became overcrowded. The cemetery was chartered in 1856.

Behind the cemetery is the Fair Grounds racetrack, organized in 1872 after the demise of the Metairie Race Course.

The Park Esplanade Apartments, overlooking the bayou, are at the right.

Bayou St. John and City Park Entrance, at Esplanade (right)

Esplanade Avenue, the tree-shaded boulevard at lower left, bridges the bayou at the entrance to City Park. Bayou St. John continues to its termination at the right in this photograph, where it once joined Carondelet's Canal, allowing shallow-draft vessels to sail from the lake to the turning basin at Basin Street.

Blanc House, Our Lady of Rosary Church, and St. Louis No. 3 Cemetery

Overlooking Bayou St. John is Blanc House, a plantation home built in about 1834 by Evariste Blanc. The house is now the rectory for Our Lady of the Rosary Church, located behind the house and facing Esplanade Avenue, which roughly parallels the bayou at this point. Across Esplanade, at left center, is the entrance to St. Louis No. 3 Cemetery, and to its right are some of the stables of the Fairgrounds Racetrack. Between the stables and Esplanade, at right center, is the Luling mansion, former headquarters of the founding organization of the Fairgrounds Racetrack, the Louisiana Jockey Club.

Dillard University (right)

In 1930 New Orleans University and Straight College merged to form Dillard University, and in 1935 moved to one of the most beautiful campuses in the South, Dillard's present location on Gentilly Road, near the Fair Grounds.

Dillard's roots extend to the period following the Civil War, when the American Missionary Association of the Congregational Church founded Straight University, and the Freedman's Aid Society of the Methodist Episcopal Church established Union Normal School, subsequently named New Orleans University.

Occupying a twenty-six-acre tract, the campus has an enrollment of 1,250.

In the background is the London Avenue outfall canal.

73

London Avenue Canal and Pumping Station

New Orleans has a total of seventeen pumping stations, designed to drain the city of its frequent subtropical rains. Much of the city is below sea level, and all of it is well below the tops of the levees that border the Mississippi River and Lake Pontchartrain. Hence, every drop of rain that leaves the city must be pumped out.

The London Avenue pumping station, shown here, drains much of the land between the Vieux Carré and the lake; it has a capacity of 4,200 cubic feet of water per second.

The drainage system, operated by the New Orleans Sewerage and Water Board since 1903, has its own power generation system, all underground transmission lines, and has a pumping capacity of 24 billion gallons per day.

City Park Entrance

At the entrance to City Park, facing Bayou St. John, is a statue of the "Great Creole," General Pierre Gustave Toutant Beauregard, who ordered the first shot fired on Fort Sumter, which began the Civil War.

Behind the statue, at the end of an avenue of oaks, is the New Orleans Museum of Art. The Dueling Oaks on the banks of Bayou Metairie, to the left of the museum, were the scene of many such "affairs of honor."

Boating in City Park (right)

On a lagoon in City Park, boaters enjoy a Sunday afternoon. In the background is McFadden House, now Christian Brothers' School for Boys.

Bayou Metairie

Along the southern boundary of City Park, paralleling City Park Avenue, is the last remnant of Bayou Metairie. The silt from its annual overflows built the high ground of Metairie Ridge. At what is now City Park, Bayou Metairie joined Bayou St. John, and also Bayou Sauvage, later called Bayou Gentilly after the road along its bank.

PART FOUR

The River and the Bayous

West Toward Metairie Along Interstate-10

In the late afternoon hours, Interstate-10 is crowded with commuters heading west toward Metairie and other suburbs in Jefferson Parish and across Lake Pontchartrain.

The cloverleaf intersection below is on the old right-of-way of the New Basin Canal. The existing drainage canal farther west is the 17th Street Canal, which drains much of Metairie and New Orleans.

The intersection at the top is with Causeway Boulevard, the approach to the Pontchartrain Causeway.

Ochsner Medical Institutions (right)

On the banks of the Mississippi, in Jefferson Parish near Causeway Boulevard, is one of the foremost medical centers in the nation, the Ochsner Medical Institutions founded by the world-famous surgeon Alton Ochsner and four associated surgeons. The institutions include the Ochsner Clinic; the Alton Ochsner Medical Foundation, which encompasses the Ochsner Foundation Hospital; the Richard W. Freeman Research Institute; and the Brent House Hotel.

Louisiana Power and Light Generating Plants, Ninemile Point

Across the river from the Ochsner Medical Institutions is a group of steam-electric generating plants at Ninemile Point, nine miles by river from downtown New Orleans, which serve Jefferson Parish and other areas adjacent to New Orleans. The first unit went on stream in 1951, and the fifth in 1973. The five plants have a total output of 1,840,000 kilowatts, making Ninemile Point the largest of Louisiana Power and Light's steam-electric generating plants.

Avondale Shipyards

Shipbuilding and marine repair are two of the major industries of the Port of New Orleans, the largest port in the United States, in terms of tonnage handled.

Towboats nudge a huge tanker into one of the docks at Avondale Shipyards, one of the area's largest employers.

Pontchartrain Causeway

Across Jefferson Parish from the Huey P. Long Mississippi River Bridge is the Pontchartrain Causeway, world's longest bridge, which connects the north shore of Lake Pontchartrain with Jefferson Parish and metropolitan New Orleans.

$46,000,000 in bonds were sold to finance the first span of the Causeway, which later was expanded to twin bridges crossing 24 miles of open water.

Metairie, Jefferson Parish, and International Airport (right)

Jefferson Parish has grown rapidly since World War II, expanding into countless acres reclaimed from the swamps west of New Orleans to become one of the state's most densely populated areas.

The Mississippi River enters this photograph at upper right, from the west, and exits at center left, heading downstream toward New Orleans.

Lafrenière Park is in the foreground at left, near Interstate-10, which roughly parallels the river, heading west toward Baton Rouge.

Above the park, in this view, and close to the river, is the New Orleans International Airport.

New Orleans International Airport

Over 6.5 million passengers use New Orleans International Airport, which provides jet service to most metropolitan areas in the Western Hemisphere.

In 1945 the airport, then called Moisant International, was constructed on 1,300 acres in the swamps of Jefferson Parish, and named in honor of John B. Moisant, aviation pioneer, who was killed in his Bleriot monoplane in 1910 near the site.

The arrival building was built in 1959 at a cost of $7,500,000, and in 1960 the first passenger jets began to operate from its runways.

Destrehan Plantation and the Destrehan Bridge
(right)

Upriver from the New Orleans International Airport is Destrehan plantation's manor house, one of the oldest houses on the Mississippi, begun in 1787.

In the background is the Destrehan bridge, scheduled for completion in 1983, and a mid-river transfer facility.

Destrehan Plantation, Looking Down River Road

The River Road, between Baton Rouge and New Orleans, was once a succession of cane fields and manor houses, which are now largely replaced by grain elevators in Destrehan's immediate area.

Bonnet Carré Spillway (right)

Designed to keep the Mississippi River at a level no higher than seventeen feet at New Orleans, where the tops of the levees are only a few feet higher, the Bonnet Carré Spillway was built in 1931 upriver from New Orleans near Destrehan to divert a maximum of a quarter of a million cubic feet of water a second into Lake Pontchartrain.

Since its construction, the two-mile-long spillway has been opened a total of seven times, the last in 1983, when this picture was taken, when the Mississippi was at its highest since 1947. After the river has settled into its bed, and the land in the spillway has dried, it becomes a prime source for fill dirt. Spillway "river sand" has provided the dirt to replace the mud of the swamps for most of the subdivisions in Metairie and Kenner, as well as for the New Orleans International Airport.

From Swamp Toward River

In a late afternoon view made from east of the Mississippi River, at about 5,000 feet above the southern edge of Lake Pontchartrain, this photograph is a microcosm of South Louisiana.

Across the top third of the picture can be seen the Mississippi, which has created the land on either side of its banks. At left is a subdivision carved from sugarcane fields on either side. In the center is the Good Hope oil field, and on the banks of the river at **right**, tank farms and oil refineries. The Bonnet Carré Spillway is at the extreme right, not yet opened in April of 1983, when this picture was made.

Generating plants near the Bonnet Carré Spillway (right)

On the west bank of the Mississippi, across from the spillway, are the Louisiana Power and Light Waterford 1 and 2 steam-electric generating plants and, toward the right, the Waterford 3 nuclear generating facility.

Downriver from the generating plants are the Hooker Chemical and Union Carbide plants on the west bank, and across the river, below the spillway, is the Shell Oil Refinery.

Twelve-Mile Bridge on Interstate-10

In the Sunday evening twilight, eastbound drivers returning to New Orleans on Interstate-10, illuminate their side of the Twelve-Mile Bridge, a name regular travelers have given this section of the elevated highway that passes over the southwestern reaches of Lake Pontchartrain.

The highway was built during the 1970s by first digging a canal through the marshes and then constructing the twin bridges with the aid of a barge-mounted crane. The crane was floated on the canal that still separates the two spans.

Logging Trails, Manchac Swamp (right)

Lying between Lake Pontchartrain (at the top) and Lake Maurepas to the west, is Manchac Swamp, a prime source for cypress around the turn of the century.

Loggers dug canals through the swamp and, at regular intervals, radiated smaller channels through the cypress forest that look like huge wagon wheels from the air. Along these channels, the cypress was floated to sawmills in the New Orleans area.

The cypress, which grows very slowly, has long since been logged out, but the radial patterns reflected in the early morning sunlight remain.

San Francisco Plantation House and Marathon Refinery

Near Garyville, on the east bank of the Mississippi about twenty miles upriver from Destrehan, is one of the most lavish plantation homes along the river, San Francisco.

Its sugar mill and fields of sugarcane have been replaced by the Marathon Oil Refinery, but the company has restored the house and grounds and maintains the house as a museum.

Manresa Retreat House

Built in 1834 as Jefferson College, Manresa Retreat House, operated by the Jesuit order, holds weekly retreats throughout the year for men of the New Orleans–Baton Rouge area.

Virtually unchanged in external appearance since its pre–Civil War days, the Manresa campus includes, at lower left, the recently restored President's House and the two guardhouses that overlook the River Road. The main Greek Revival building is in the center, with its Gothic chapel at the right, and the dining hall and priests' residence at the rear. There are three avenues of live oaks on the property, one on either side of the main building at the front, and the other in the center at the rear.

L'Hermitage

Built for a young Creole, Michel Douradou Bringier, who fought alongside Andrew Jackson on the Plains of Chalmette in the War of 1812, the Hermitage was named after General Jackson's Nashville, Tennessee, residence.

In 1959 Dr. Robert C. Judice, a young New Orleans physician, and his wife began a detailed restoration of the house, saving it for future generations.

In the background is the Mississippi, which still winds around Bringier Point, across the river from Donaldsonville and the first great fork of the Mississippi, Bayou Lafourche.

Madewood and Bayou Lafourche (right)

Built of timber hewn on the plantation, by a North Carolinian, Colonel Thomas Pugh, in the 1840s, Madewood was restored in 1965 by Mrs. Harold K. Marshall of New Orleans, who with her son has turned the great house into an internationally known cultural center, home of the Madewood Arts Festival.

Bayou Lafourche is no longer the impressive stream it must have been in the 1800s, its junction with the Mississippi having been blocked by a levee about the turn of the century. Now much smaller than it was during the steamboat age, the stream was then known as the longest Main Street in the world.

Laurel Valley

Another of the great plantations along Bayou La-fourche was Laurel Valley, near Thibodaux, the largest surviving nineteenth-century sugar plantation complex in the South. Built in 1840, Laurel Valley changed hands a number of times until it was purchased by the J. Wilson Lepine family in 1893, which still retains ownership.

The remains of the sugar mill, damaged by Hurricane Betsy in 1965, still stand at right, along with rows of cabins, built before the Civil War.

Shrimp Boats Near Golden Meadow (right)

Nearing the Gulf of Mexico at Golden Meadow, the character of Bayou Lafourche changes. Land alongside the bayou is too narrow for sugar plantations, but provides a safe anchorage for the shrimp boat owners who have plied the coastal waters for generations.

In more recent years, workboats serving the offshore oil industry have added much to the lower Bayou Lafourche economy.

Grand Isle and Fort Livingston

Two of Louisiana's barrier islands, Grand Isle and Grand Terre, form part of the seaside boundary of Barataria Bay, back door to New Orleans, where the pirates of Jean Lafitte were based before the War of 1812.

The British met with Lafitte to request his aid in guiding their army through the swamps to New Orleans. He refused, and he told Louisiana's Governor William C. C. Claiborne of their $30,000 offer. However, the United States Navy, under orders to clear the seas of the pirates, attacked Lafitte's stronghold on Grand Terre Island, and chased him and his men into the swamp. Fortunately, Andrew Jackson was able to enlist Lafitte's aid for the Battle of New Orleans.

Fort Livingston was built on the western end of Grand Terre as part of the coastal defenses of New Orleans after the War of 1812, but today it is deserted.

The Mississippi Meets Blue Water (right)

From 10,000 feet above the Gulf of Mexico, the crisp, sharp line between the muddy waters of the Mississippi and the deep blue waters of the Gulf is as unexpected as it is obvious.

In the background is part of Southwest Pass at left, South Pass in the center, and Southeast Pass at the right.

West Across Mouth of the Mississippi

The mouth of Mississippi was an unpredictable barrier, rather than a passageway, until the 1880s, when Captain James B. Eads designed a series of jetties that forced the river to clear its own channel into the Gulf, and provide deep-draft vessels year-round access to New Orleans. In the foreground is Pass a Loutre, North Pass, pursuing an unfettered course to the sea. In the background is Southwest Pass, which extends far into the Gulf along jetties designed by Captain Eads.

Upriver Toward Forts Jackson and St. Philip
(right)

Below Fort St. Philip, on the east bank of the Mississippi, at right, the riverbank is unprotected by a levee, and allows the river to continue its age-old practice of spilling over the banks, dropping much of its burden of sand and silt, and building more land.

Fort St. Philip was founded by the Spanish in 1786 on the site of an earlier fortification, and Fort Jackson, across the river on its west bank, was completed in 1832. The twin forts formed the first and principal line of defense for New Orleans during the Civil War, and were subject to a ninety-six-hour bombardment by Admiral David G. Farragut's forty-ship armada in April of 1862.

After cutting a chain stretched across the river between the two forts, the Yankee fleet sailed to New Orleans unopposed, and the city quickly capitulated.

Fort Jackson

Fort Jackson remained in active service through the Spanish-American War, when heavier coastal guns were installed, and World War I, when it served as a training base. It was deactivated in 1920, and now is part of a park and museum complex operated by Plaquemines Parish.

Southward Toward the Gulf

Residents on the west bank of the Mississippi upriver from Empire are protected from the waters of the river by a levee along its banks, at left, and from storm tides from the Gulf by another levee at the right. Louisiana Highway 23 parallels the river below New Orleans, and offers an escape route to higher ground upriver in the event of a hurricane warning.

Port Sulphur

Sulphur, deep beneath the marshes southwest of Port Sulphur, is melted with superheated water and pumped to Port Sulphur, where it cools and hardens into huge blocks prior to shipment.

Bayou Barataria (right)

West of the Mississippi River, closer to New Orleans, is Bayou Barataria, best known as the lair of Lafitte and his pirates. Now visited daily by cruise boats touring the swamp, Barataria and Lafitte, towns along the bayou, are inhabited by descendants of those early denizens of the swamps, who now are employed primarily in the seafood and offshore oil industries.

English Turn

In 1699 Jean Baptiste le Moyne, Sieur de Bienville, to be known as the founder of New Orleans, encountered a twelve-gun British corvette at a great bend in the Mississippi below the location he had chosen to become *Nouvelle Orléans.*

The British had planned to establish a settlement near the mouth of the river, and Captain Lewis Banks was searching for a proper location. Bienville promptly sailed up to the ship and announced that the corvette was in French territory; that the British must leave immediately or he would set his own fleet, located just upriver, upon them. Although Bienville had no fleet at all, and no settlement, the British believed him. They turned around and sailed back down to the Gulf of Mexico, prompting the name "English Turn."

Fort Pike

Although no shot was ever fired in battle, Fort Pike was built following the War of 1812 to defend one of the eastern approaches to New Orleans, the Rigolets, a relatively narrow waterway between Lake Pontchartrain and the Gulf of Mexico.

The road that passes the fort, now a state commemorative area, is U.S. Highway 90, the Chef Menteur Highway, which leads west from this point toward New Orleans.

Fishing Camps, Chef Menteur Highway

Fishing camps, year-round residences for some, and only summer places for others, face Lake Pontchartrain toward the west, at the bottom of the picture, and Lake Catherine toward the east.

Beauregard House and Chalmette Battlefield, Looking Upriver Toward New Orleans (right)

In the foreground is the eastern end of the Plains of Chalmette, site of General Andrew Jackson's command of Tennesseeans, Creoles, and pirates, who defeated the pride of the British army in 1815 in the final battle of the War of 1812.

Now a national park, the battlefield and river are provided an overlook from a monument at right. Beauregard House, a plantation home on the riverbank, built well after the battle, serves as the park's headquarters. Beauregard House was the last home of Judge René Beauregard, son of the Confederate general.

Jackson Barracks

Between St. Claude Avenue and the Mississippi, downriver from the city itself, is Jackson Barracks, built to house the federal garrison at New Orleans in the 1830s, and completed during Andrew Jackson's presidency (1829–1837).

Called "the finest complex of Greek Revival buildings existing in Louisiana," the post was a general hospital and an embarkation point during the Mexican War, and was occupied by both Confederate and federal troops during the Civil War.

Jackson Barracks presently serves as headquarters for the Louisiana National Guard.

The Natchez *Below Downtown New Orleans* (right)

Looking upriver toward the Central Business District and the Vieux Carré, the east bank is on the right, and Algiers Point, on the left, is on the west bank.

The river is 2,200 feet wide at the foot of Canal Street, with a bankside depth of thirty to sixty feet, and a depth in midstream of from 100 to 180 feet.

PART FIVE

Festive New Orleans

Lee Circle on Mardi Gras Day, 1983 (left)

In the spring of 1699, searching for the main course of the Mississippi River, Iberville's expedition camped on the banks of a small bayou near the mouth of the river. It was Mardi Gras night, and the bayou was named Bayou Mardi Gras. New Orleans and Mardi Gras have been intimately associated ever since.

Mardi Gras, or Fat Tuesday, the day before Ash Wednesday and the beginning of the Lenten season, has been traditionally celebrated since medieval times in Europe, but New Orleans did not hold its first costume parade until 1827. The first Carnival floats made their appearance in 1838, and the city's first torchlight parade in 1857.

During the final eleven days of the Carnival season, between the twelfth day after Christmas and the day before Lent, more than fifty parades are held, more than sixty balls are staged, and over a million dollars worth of trinkets are thrown to the crowds.

On Mardi Gras Day, more than a half-million people line the parade routes through the city, with most concentrated around Canal and St. Charles, to see and participate in "the greatest free show on earth."

Gallier Hall, Lafayette Square (right)

117

Rex Reviewing Stand, Pickwick Club, St. Charles and Canal

Canal Street, Basin Street, and Loyola Avenue on Mardi Gras Day (right)

The Jazz Festival

During two weeks every May, a quarter-million people attend weekend performances of the New Orleans Jazz Festival held at the Fair Grounds Racetrack, and at other locations about the city.

The music can satisfy nearly any taste, since performing groups range from Dixieland to Progressive, and from Latin to Gospel, in a celebration that continues the traditions of one of America's most interesting cities.

Louis Armstrong Park and Performing Arts Theater at Twilight

The Steamer *President* Begins Moonlight Cruise During Jazz Festival (right)

The *Mississippi Queen* Begins Cruise Upriver

Above the Greater New Orleans Bridge, the *Natchez* (left), the *Mississippi Queen* (extreme right)

Central Business District from Above Loyola (left)

Canal Street (above)

Bourbon Street

Riverfront—Poydras and Canal (right)

130

A Note on the Photography

Aerial photography presents another whole set of problems in addition to the perennial questions one faces on the ground, and southern Louisiana adds its own complications of humidity, haze, and unpredictable thunderheads.

On the ground in architectural photography, for example, I will determine the right time of day and time of year to photograph a structure, and more often than not compensate for the excessive contrast inherent in nature's lighting of the subject.

In the air the reverse is usually true; there is not enough contrast. And the higher one flies, the less there is, so if one uses a soft, long-scale film successfully on the ground, he will probably be disappointed with it in the air.

In addition to the lack of contrast, there is the continually frustrating, ever-present haze, particularly over the metropolitan areas, which makes a big difference between a clear day on the ground and a clear day in the air. I have canceled a number of assignments because, even though it seemed a good day on the ground, in the air it was another story. The haze turns everything blue, and in color, there's really not much one can do about it. In black and white, an orange or red filter will cut through a lot of haze, but orange filters do not work too well in color.

Along with the haze itself and its limits on visibility, the relationship between the camera and the sun affects the overall color balance of the scene.

As we fly around a target area, the color balance shifts from "normal" with the sun over my shoulder (where the light is most uninteresting) to a predominant blue as I shoot into the sun. I can compensate to some extent by using slightly yellow filters, but the problem is that we're constantly moving, and the color balance is constantly shifting.

For this reason, I chose to use color negative, rather than color transparency material, and adjusted the color balance of the print. Kodacolor II was my mainstay for all the aerial work, except for low-light situations when I switched to Kodacolor 400. All color separations were made from 11×14-inch prints.

Aircraft are not permitted to fly low over populated areas, and in locales where I wanted a dramatic roof-top view, I resorted to a "bucket truck" similar to those the power companies use to repair their lines. This allowed a 65-foot elevation, enough to see over the French Quarter roof-tops, which seldom reach beyond fifty feet.

Another problem in the air is vibration, whether in a fixed-wing craft, a helicopter, or a bucket truck. The photographer must learn to insulate his camera from it, floating it in his arms and hands, rather than bracing it on his chest, shoulder, cheekbone, or tripod as he learned to do on the ground. A fast shutter speed is an essential, and, within reason, the larger and heavier the camera the better.

Although I began research and exploratory photography in 1981, my serious shooting commenced Mardi Gras Day, February 15, 1983, and continued into the month of June.

Index